Roscoe:

A Respectable Dog
with Good Moral Principles

James L. "Johnny Ray" Thompson

Roscoe: A Respectable Dog with Good Moral Principles
Copyright © 2017 by James L. "Johnny Ray" Thompson

ISBN-13: Paperback: 978-1-64045-302-9
         PDF: 978-1-64045-303-6
         ePub: 978-1-64045-304-3
         Kindle: 978-1-64045-305-0

Printed in the United States of America

LitFire
PUBLISHING

LitFire LLC
1-800-511-9787
www.litfirepublishing.com

order@litfirepublishing.com

Acknowledgements

This book is dedicated to the memory of my daddy Mr. Theo Thompson, Sr., the one who gave me permission to own a dog and who helped me, financially, take care of him despite the fact that my mother vowed that no dog would be brought to our house. Also, I would like to give a superb dedication to the memory of my neighbor Mr. Willie B. Lambert, the man who let me keep Roscoe, my very first dog, in his backyard and inside a doghouse that he had stopped using many years prior to Roscoe's arrival therefore providing a safe and secure home that was located just a few houses down the street for my dog. For this great favor, I must say, "Thank you Bee." Moreover, I would like to make a special dedication to the memory of Miss Zella Hankins, another one of my neighbors who lived right next door to Mr. Lambert and who yelled at me one morning for whipping Roscoe for not obeying my crazy commands. Zella, for asking me didn't I know that there were laws against being cruel to animals and causing me to stop the frivolous beating of my dog, I must say, "Thank you too." As a ten-year-old child at the time, I didn't know that there were laws against being cruel to animals, but I do now. Again, thank you very much.

Kenneth Undre Thompson

Moreover, I would like to give another superb dedication to the memory of my nephew, Kenneth Undre Thompson, who was also a victim of domestic violence by being shot and killed by his live-in girlfriend. At the time, they had a nine-month-old baby daughter. Now, may all four of you good people rest in peace.

Carnell Thompson and Roscoe

This is a book of nonfiction.

Therefore, everything that I've said in it about my first dog, Roscoe, is factual.

While in the fifth grade, ten-year-old Johnny Ray Thompson walked to and from school daily. He soon noticed while going through some of the neighborhoods that there were dogs that would start barking and chasing after him. Holding his books under one arm, Johnny Ray had to run from these dogs each morning and each evening after his school had dismissed.

Sometimes when these dogs would be chasing him, Johnny Ray noticed that there were children around his age shouting to their dogs, "Get him! Get him!" And, this bad behavior of the children made him really mad. He just couldn't understand how someone could tell a dog to bite anybody.

So, Johnny Ray stopped going through these neighborhoods alone. After having been chased by these bad-biting dogs a few times, he would wait and get another neighbor or friend to walk with him. And, now the both of them carried a stick or some rocks to throw at the dogs instead of continuing to run from them.

As time passed on, Johnny Ray wanted his own dog very badly. But, he wanted his own dog for the wrong reason; he wanted a bad-biting and aggressive dog, so that he could train his dog into being a vicious dog in trying to attack some of the other children in his neighborhood. One day while his daddy was looking at TV and resting on their sofa, Johnny Ray asked his daddy could he get a dog.

"Johnny Ray, it's alright with me", his daddy said, "you also need to go in there and ask your mother and see what she says about it." Then, he went into their kitchen where his mother was cooking the family supper. "Mama, can I have a dog," Johnny Ray said. "No!", his mother said, "no dog is coming to this house, and I don't care what your daddy says." His mother continued to stir the food in the boiler she had on the stove and ignored Johnny Ray afterwards.

Now, Johnny Ray had a serious problem. His daddy didn't mind letting him own a dog for a pet, but his mother didn't want a dog at their home. He had to find a place to keep his dog before he got one. So, he went walking through his neighborhood to see who he could ask for help in this matter.

Within walking just a few feet away from his house, Johnny Ray met one of his neighbors who had been a close friend to his family for many years. This neighbor's name was Mr. Willie B. Lambert. Mr. Lambert was just walking on this particular afternoon for his daily exercise. Bee, as he was affectionately called in the community by all of the grownups, was wearing overalls and a wide straw hat when Johnny Ray approached him and said, "Mr. Bee, if I get me a dog can I keep him in your backyard?" "Sure, Johnny Ray," Mr. Lambert said, "because the last hunting dog, Blue Doe, that I had died many years ago. But, I still have his doghouse, and you are more than welcome to use it. But tell me why you don't want to keep him at your house." "My mama want let me," Johnny Ray said. "Well, I sure am sorry to hear of that. Of course, you know that you will be responsible for taking care of your own dog, don't you?", Mr. Lambert said. "Yes, Sir", Johnny Ray said, "thank you very much." Johnny Ray ran back home and told his daddy what Mr. Lambert had told him.

After Johnny Ray had made it back home and told his daddy that Mr. Bee had given him permission to keep a dog at his house, his daddy, while pointing his finger at Johnny Ray said, "Alright, are willing to feed, water, and take care of a dog when you get one?" "Yes, Sir," Johnny Ray said. "Did you thank Mr. Bee for letting you keep a dog in his backyard?", his daddy also asked. "Yes, Sir", Johnny Ray also said to his daddy. "Well, find you a puppy, and I'll buy the food for it", his daddy said.

A few days later, Johnny Ray had gone a few blocks from his house to play with his friend Marshall Lane, Jr. While playing basketball with Marshall, Johnny Ray noticed that Marshall's next-door- neighbor owned a German Shepherd dog that had just had a litter of puppies. Now, the German Shepherd dog had always been Johnny Ray's favorite breed or kind of dog since he was a very small child in head start because this was the kind of dog that the police used in doing their work. Also, this kind of dog had a known reputation for being very intelligent and very easily to train, especially for being protective of its owner and for guiding blind people. So, Johnny Ray wanted to get and raise one of these puppies very badly because he wanted to train his dog to be very vicious. Moreover, Johnny Ray asked Marshall how many puppies did his neighbor's dog have. Marshall told Johnny Ray that his neighbor's dog had nine puppies. And, he told Johnny Ray that his neighbor, an old lady, had said that whenever the puppies got old enough to be taken away from their mother to a new home, she was going to give them all away to whomever wanted one of them.

After hearing what his friend Marshall had just told him about these pretty puppies of various colors, Johnny Ray didn't believe Marshall, so he went next door and asked Marshall's neighbor about the puppies to make sure that his friend wasn't playing a trick on him. "Sure, Son", the old lady said to Johnny Ray, "you can have one of those puppies. They are too young to leave their mother now. You just come back to me in about two more weeks, and I'll let you pick you one out of the litter." "Thank you very much," Johnny Ray told the lady. Johnny Ray was so excited about hearing this good news. In fact, he was so excited about being told that he could have one of the puppies that he told Marshall that he didn't want to play any more basketball, and then he ran home to tell his daddy the good news.

When Johnny Ray made it home, he saw his daddy working in the family garden. "Hey, Daddy, guess what," yelled Johnny Ray "the lady on East Academy Street got some puppies, and she said that she will give me one in about two more weeks." "She did," said his daddy, "well, that's good in her to do that. What kind of dog is it?" "Half German Shepherd and something else," said Johnny Ray. "Now, you do understand that you will be taking care of that dog, don't you," said his daddy. "Yes, sir," said Johnny Ray. The next day Johnny Ray went to school. And, during recess, and while playing a game of marbles, he told his friends that he would be getting a dog of his own in two weeks. His friends were so surprised, and they were happy for him. Some of his friends said that they would ask their parents if they could have their very own dog.

After the two-week time period of waiting to get his dog had come to an end, Johnny Ray went to the old lady's house to get his dog. After knocking on her door a few times, the old lady came outside, and Johnny Ray told her that he had come to get one of the puppies that her dog had had. "Come on around here to the backyard and pick you out one," said the old lady. Once in the backyard, Johnny Ray saw all of the puppies and their mother under the old lady's house. To him, all of the puppies were so fat and pretty, and it was hard for him to decide which one he wanted. "Do you see one that you really like," the old lady asked. "Yes, Ma'am," said Johnny Ray, "I want that solid black one on the end over there, while pointing at the puppy that he had chosen. And I hope he is a boy." "Well, let me take the mother dog inside, so that she won't be able to attack you when you pick your puppy up into your arms," the old lady said. Once the old lady had taken the mother dog and put her inside of her house, Johnny Ray grabbed the black puppy and looked very carefully at it. "Wow, it's a boy," Johnny Ray shouted!

Then, he started walking home with his puppy. As he passed the front of the old lady's house, he thanked her again for giving him his puppy. The puppy was so fat, cute, and black, but yet he was still small enough that Johnny Ray could hold in one of the palms of one of his hands and carry him. As the puppy started whining, Johnny Ray started rubbing his head. Also, he started talking to his puppy and calling him by his name, Roscoe. He got this name from one of his older cousins who had once owned a dog by the name of Roscoe which was a very vicious dog and was a well-trained dog by his cousin Eddie.

What Johnny Ray liked most about Eddie's dog was the fact that whenever his cousin Eddie would shout, "Get him, Roscoe," his dog would attack whomever he told him to get. Moreover, when Johnny Ray made it home with his puppy, his daddy was sitting in their backyard. "Daddy, here he is," said Johnny Ray. "Yeah, and I got this for you," said his daddy while simultaneously showing Johnny Ray a new chain and collar that he had just bought Johnny Ray for his puppy. "Thank you, daddy," shouted Johnny Ray! His daddy had also bought some dog food and a bottle to feed Roscoe with. Then, they walked and carried Roscoe to Mr. Lambert's house to his new home. They fed him, and then they put him up for the night.

As time passed on, Roscoe grew, and he grew, and he grew. Around three months old, Roscoe had grown into a huge puppy. Whenever Johnny Ray would walk him on his leash, Roscoe would pull Johnny Ray and sometimes drag him through the neighborhood.

Since so many of his friends and neighbors kept asking him what kind of dog Roscoe was because he was growing so fast, Johnny Ray went back to the old lady that had given Roscoe to him, and he asked her what kind of dog was Roscoe's father. "Son, your dog's daddy is that big brown lab across the street over there," the old lady told Johnny Ray, " he should be a smart dog when he gets grown because German Shepherds and Labs are both real smart dogs." Now, Johnny Ray wanted to know what kind of dog was a Lab. So, he started asking some of the older people that were in his neighborhood. One man told him that Lab was short for Labrador Retriever. "Labrador Retrievers are smart dogs that are mostly used for hunting," said the older man.

The man also told Johnny Ray, "You can train those dogs to do just about anything that you want them to do." After finding out that Roscoe was half German Shepherd and half Labrador Retriever, and that both of these dogs were known for being very easily to train, Johnny Ray quickly decided that it was time to start training Roscoe. In addition, the very next day after school, he got Roscoe's leash and he took Roscoe for a walk. Each time he would approach some of the other children, Johnny Ray would jerk the leash forward toward the other children and shout, "Get him, Roscoe!" But, Roscoe wouldn't even go towards the children. Instead, Roscoe would just turn his head and look back at Johnny Ray. Johnny Ray tried to make Roscoe bite the children several times, but each time he tried Roscoe just looked at his master.

When Roscoe didn't obey Johnny Ray's commands to attack and bite the children, Johnny Ray got real mad at Roscoe and took him back to the doghouse. After getting Roscoe back home to his doghouse, Johnny Ray hitched Roscoe back to the log chain that he had the other end of fastened to the big old tree that was located beside Roscoe's doghouse. Then, he got a small stick, and he started whipping and shouting at Roscoe. "When I say get him, I mean get him," Johnny Ray shouted! Roscoe was howling very loudly because Johnny Ray was hitting him very hard with the stick, and he was in much pain. Little did he know, this was not the right way to train a dog or any animal. However, he continued to whip Roscoe for about two full minutes until Mr. Lambert's next-door neighbor, Miss Zella Hankins, told him to stop whipping Roscoe, and she asked him didn't he know that there were laws against being cruel to animals. Now, this really scared Johnny Ray and he didn't answer Miss Hankins because he just knew that Miss Hankins would tell his mother about him whipping Roscoe when she and his mother met again at church on Sunday. Also, he thought that she would call the police on him since she had mentioned about the laws of being cruel to animals to him. So, he just quietly walked back home. Later into the afternoon, and just before dark had come, Johnny Ray took Roscoe some food and water.

After feeding him, he sat with Roscoe for a while, and he rubbed and massaged Roscoe's back before leaving him for the night. In addition, he told Roscoe that he was sorry for whipping him. "You did right by not biting those children when I wanted you to," he told Roscoe. As he walked back to his parents' house, Johnny Ray began to feel very sad and guilty about whipping his dog earlier. When he had washed his hands and eaten his supper, Johnny Ray took his bath and went to bed. But, before he had gotten into his bed, he got down on his knees, and he said his prayers. While saying his prayers, he asked God to forgive him for being so mean and cruel to his dog, and he quickly decided not to ever whip Roscoe again.

And he never did whip Roscoe anymore. Furthermore, he started trying to think of something else that maybe he could train Roscoe to do. As he lay in his bed with his hands behind his head, he continued to think extremely hard on this matter. After thinking for quite some time and not coming up with an answer, Johnny Ray fell asleep.

Within a few more months, Johnny Ray was really enjoying his dog. By now, Roscoe was about ten months old, and he had really grown into a large dog. And, Johnny Ray was really proud to walk with him on his side of town.

Whenever there weren't any people on the ball diamond that was located behind Johnny Ray's house, he would take Roscoe to the diamond and teach him how to fetch a ball, stick, or whatever he threw away from himself. Roscoe was excellent at fetching whatever he would throw. And whenever he would fake a throw of a ball or stick, Roscoe would just sit and look to see if he could see it falling to the ground. If he couldn't see the object, he would just turn and look at Johnny Ray. Sometimes if Johnny Ray was holding the object behind him, Roscoe would go behind him and sniff his hands. Later, Johnny Ray taught Roscoe how to sit, lie down, to stay in place whenever he would walk all the way down to the other end of the baseball diamond, and to do handshakes; four more tricks that he performed really well whenever he was asked to do them. Also, there were times when Johnny Ray and Roscoe would be on the ball diamond practicing Roscoe's tricks, and some of the other children in the neighborhood would come out where they were and just sit and watch Roscoe do whatever he was asked to do by his master. It didn't take very long before more and more children started coming to the baseball diamond whenever they saw Johnny Ray out there with Roscoe. Johnny Ray didn't ever let the other children play with Roscoe, but he would let Roscoe give them a handshake occasionally.

These children really enjoyed seeing Roscoe obey Johnny Ray as if he were another human being doing exactly what he was told to do by his parents. At first, many of them couldn't believe what they were seeing. They were going home telling their family members and other friends. Consequently, this started some of the parents and other grownups to coming to see Roscoe perform his tricks. Roscoe was really a smart and very obedient dog.

Although it appeared at first that all of Johnny Ray's neighbors really enjoyed seeing him practice and train Roscoe in the afternoons on the ball diamond, this wasn't true. Showing off Roscoe's intelligence made some of them extremely jealous. For example, there was one neighbor who lived about four houses down the street from Johnny Ray. His name was Jeff. And, he owned a dog by the name of Max. Max was older than Roscoe, but he wasn't as big as Roscoe. Also, Max was really bad about trying to bite people. And, he was a black and tan colored hound dog. One day Jeff brought Max to the ball diamond, and he told Johnny Ray that Max could whip Roscoe in fighting. Jeff didn't like the fact that Roscoe was smart and many people were coming to see him, so he disliked Roscoe and wanted his dog to fight him. Johnny Ray told Jeff that he didn't want Roscoe fighting. "Why? Are you scared Max will kill that mutt," Jeff said while laughing. "No, I just don't want my dog fighting at all," Johnny Ray shouted at Jeff! Quickly, Johnny Ray put Roscoe back on his leash and took him home. However, the very next day Jeff brought his dog, Max, to the ball diamond to fight Roscoe again. This time Jeff brought Max up in Roscoe's face and told Max, "Get him!" At this point Max attacked Roscoe, and Johnny Ray shouted, "Get him, Roscoe!" These dogs started fighting very hard. They were really growling and chewing on each other. Then, all of a sudden, Roscoe grabbed Max by the throat and flipped him on the ground real fast. And Roscoe just held Max by his throat while slowly choking him to death. "Make him stop! Please, Johnny Ray, make Roscoe stop. Your dog is the best," shouted Jeff! "Stop Roscoe," Johnny Ray said. And, then Roscoe released Max, and when he did Max ran back home with his tail between his legs. All of the other children laughed at Jeff and pointed at Max while he was running home after just having been beaten up by Roscoe. Jeff was so ashamed.

After Roscoe had whipped Max really good and caused him to start bleeding, the word soon spread all over the town of Canton, Mississippi that Johnny Ray had a real good fighting dog. Then, a few other boys wanted to bring their dogs to fight Roscoe, but Johnny Ray would always tell them no because he didn't want Roscoe to get hurt.

In addition, and unexpectedly just like the previous dog fight with Max, another boy by the name of James brought his dog a few days later to the ball diamond to fight Roscoe. Now James was older than Johnny Ray, about four years. He was a teenager. "I bet that mutt you got won't win a fight against my dog, Butch," James said. Now, James had a pretty black and white collie dog. "James, take your dog on somewhere else because I don't want Roscoe fighting anymore. But by this time, James picked his dog, Butch, up and threw him on Roscoe and said, "Get him, Butch!" Now, the fight was on. "Get him, Roscoe," Johnny Ray said. These dogs were really fighting. And this fight was more exciting than the first fight because Roscoe and Butch were standing up on their hind legs, and they were really growling and gnawing on each other. And, just like the previous fight with Max, the hound dog, Roscoe grabbed Butch by his throat, and he didn't let go. At this point, Butch started whining because he was being choked to death. "Johnny Ray, stop Roscoe. Your dog is the best. Please stop him," James said.

Slowly, Johnny Ray walked up to both dogs, and he hitched Roscoe's leash to his collar, and he pulled Roscoe off of Butch. However, in this particular fight Roscoe had gotten some deep cuts on his neck, and he was bleeding just like Butch was, although he did win this fight too. Johnny Ray took Roscoe back home and washed the blood off of him before his daddy had seen Roscoe with the blood all over him.

Since Roscoe had now proven to the other dog owners that he could kill their dogs if his master, Johnny Ray, had wanted him to, the other dog owners became very afraid of letting their dogs fight him. Moreover, it would be a little over three months before anyone else would want to bring his dog on the ball diamond to fight Roscoe. And, when this time did come, it was another boy by the name of Dennis. Dennis had a big black and tan colored German Shepherd by the name of Trixie. Trixie was a girl dog, and she was a pretty dog. Dennis lived on the west side of Canton. One day at school, and during recess, Dennis walked up to Johnny Ray, and he said, "Johnny Ray, I heard that you have a dog that can really fight. Well, if he is so good at fighting let's see if he can whip my dog Trixie." Johnny Ray told Dennis that he didn't want to fight Roscoe anymore. "Why? Are you chicken? Your dog whipped up on those little dogs, but let's see if he can handle Trixie. I know that Trixie will kill him if I don't get her off of him," Dennis said. "Your dog will be just like the other two that Roscoe whipped," Johnny Ray said to Dennis. "Well, if you are not a chicken, and so sure of what your dog can do let's let them fight," Dennis said. "I don't want my dog fighting anymore," Johnny Ray said again to Dennis. "Chicken, chicken, chicken," cried Dennis.

And, this really made Johnny Ray mad. "Okay! Since you say I'm chicken, let's let them fight on Saturday at twelve o'clock noon," said Johnny Ray. "Alright with me. Trixie and I will be there on the ball diamond at exactly twelve o'clock noon Saturday," said Dennis. This conversation took place on Wednesday, and the rest of the week at school several students were talking about the fight that was going to take place at the ball diamond the following Saturday between Roscoe and Trixie. Also, all of the students that had seen the fights between Roscoe and Max and Roscoe and Butch were saying that Roscoe was sure going to whip Trixie, a girl dog. They were very very confident that this fight between Roscoe and Trixie would be an easy win for Roscoe. Finally, Saturday had come, and Johnny Ray and Roscoe were waiting at twelve o'clock noon for Dennis and Trixie to appear. Since Dennis and his dog were a little late coming, many of the onlookers began to say that Dennis had chickened out of the fight. But about ten minutes after twelve o'clock noon, Dennis and his dog, Trixie, did appear on the ball diamond. "We still have time to call this fight off," Johnny Ray said to Dennis. "I'm not calling nothing off. My dog will kill that mutt," said Dennis to Johnny Ray.

While Johnny Ray and Dennis were talking, Roscoe walked up to Trixie and began to sniff all around her. When it was decided between Johnny Ray and Dennis that this fight would still go on as planned, Dennis placed Trixie directly in front of Roscoe and shouted, "Get him!" And, at this point, Trixie attacked Roscoe. But for some strange reason Roscoe wouldn't fight Trixie. "Get him, Roscoe," yelled Johnny Ray. But again and again after each attack by Trixie, Roscoe just wouldn't fight Trixie. Johnny Ray didn't understand what was going on with his dog. All of the onlookers started laughing at Roscoe and Johnny Ray. Soon, Johnny Ray decided to take Roscoe back home. He told Dennis that something was wrong, and that Roscoe would fight Trixie later. Dennis said, while laughing at Johnny Ray, "Yeah, that mutt is scared of Trixie." "Time will tell about that," Johnny Ray told Dennis. The following Monday and while at school, Johnny Ray and Dennis met, and they decided that they would let Roscoe and Trixie fight again. After this rematch between these same two dogs had been scheduled for the next Saturday at the same time, Johnny Ray came up with a plan that he just knew would get Roscoe to fight Trixie and whip her good. He knew that Roscoe didn't like for anyone, not even him, to get close to his dog bowl while he was eating because Roscoe had growled very meanly at him several times before, warning him not to bother his dog bowl while he was eating. So, he quickly decided that on the day of the fight, he would make sure that Roscoe would be hungry, and that he would bring his food and water on the ball diamond and feed him there. And, if Trixie went near his dog bowl Roscoe would warn her first, and if she continued to eat his food then he would attack her and give her a good whipping.

In addition, and just a few days later, it was Saturday, the day of the rematch fight between Roscoe and Trixie. To ensure that this would be a good fight this time between these two dogs, Johnny Ray made sure that he didn't feed Roscoe any food at all the previous Friday afternoon. Around eleven forty-five a.m. on this particular Saturday morning, Johnny Ray took Roscoe's food and water to the baseball diamond and placed it under a pecan tree. Several other children were already at the pecan tree waiting to see the big fight. Also, he told the children not to bother the food and water, and not to let another animal or person bother it either. Then, he went to Mr. Lambert's house and got Roscoe and took him to the ball diamond and waited for Dennis and Trixie. After about fifteen minutes of waiting for Dennis and Trixie, they appeared with Dennis having a big smile on his face. When they had gotten almost upon Roscoe and Johnny Ray, Johnny Ray took Roscoe to his food and started letting him eat his food. Dennis brought Trixie right up to Roscoe and told Trixie to, "Get him!" Again, Trixie attacked Roscoe and did some loud growling, and Roscoe backed away from his food. Each time that he tried to come back to his dog bowl, Trixie would growl real loud, and he would turn away again. "Get her, Roscoe," shouted Johnny Ray! But Roscoe didn't attempt to fight her. In fact, Trixie ate just about all of Roscoe's food.

The other children laughed again at Johnny Ray and Roscoe. Trixie did leave a little of the food in Roscoe's dog bowl, and Roscoe ate it. Since he was so young and didn't know much about dogs, Johnny Ray just didn't understand why Roscoe didn't fight her.

Later that Saturday night while he and his daddy were talking, Johnny Ray asked his daddy why Roscoe would fight a boy dog and wouldn't fight a girl dog. "Son, Roscoe has some respect about himself. And, you should be just like your dog when it comes to girls. Little boys shouldn't ever fight girls. And, grown men should never fight women. "But today she ate his food, and he still didn't fight her," said Johnny Ray to his daddy. "So what! He was just being a gentleman just like you should be with girls. Always respect girls and women, Johnny Ray," his daddy shouted! "What if she hits me first," said Johnny Ray. "You go and tell your teacher if you are at school, and if you are at home you go and tell her mother or tell me or your mother," his daddy said. "But Daddy, Roscoe won't bite the other children when I tell him to," Johnny Ray said. "Why you want that dog to bite the other children," his daddy shouted, "I better not hear of you trying to make that dog bite any of these other children around here. If I do, I'm going to whip you good.

And, stop trying to fight that dog. How would you like it if someone were taking you around and making you fight other boys and getting cuts and bruises on you," his daddy also shouted! "Okay, Daddy, I hear you," said Johnny Ray. "Johnny Ray, his daddy said while pointing his finger at Johnny Ray, "you have a fine dog. He just gave you a good example today as to how you are to respect all women and girls. When you get grown and get a wife or a girlfriend, don't you ever fight her. I have never hit your mother. That dog that you have got more respect about himself than the average grown man does. Today, the laugh wasn't on Roscoe; but on all of those people who came to see a boy dog fight a girl dog. They all should've been ashamed of themselves, especially the grown folks that were out there. But Roscoe showed them. He showed them that he has more respect for himself than many of them do.

Above all, he showed all of you that were out there on that diamond today that he's a respectable dog with good moral principles.

Afterword

To the readers of this book, let's face the facts about an extremely dangerous epidemic disease that's not caused by a virus. This disease is caused primarily by ignorance. This disease that I am referring to is known as Domestic Violence. The moral of this book is to teach young school-age kids as early as possible that domestic violence is wrong, and it is against the law. Also, I wrote this book to show every child, man, and woman of age to understand that if a dog can show love and respect for a female dog, surely men can show love and positive respect for women; if they are trained properly. Human beings are supposed to be the highest intelligent animals on earth. But why can't we conduct ourselves like we are when it comes to our spouses and other intimate friends? Just to further show just how bad and widespread domestic violence is in our own supposed to be civilized country, consider the following frightening facts about it:

1. Every nine seconds, a woman in the United States of America is assaulted or beaten, according to the National Coalition Against Domestic Violence.

2. One in three women, 33%, and one in four men, 25%, have been victims of physical violence by an intimate partner.

3. Women between twenty-five and thirty-four years of age are reportedly the most vulnerable to partner violence.

4. Forty-five percent of female rape victims were raped by an intimate partner.

5. Only thirty-four percent of people injured by an intimate partner receive medical care for their injuries.

6. According to the Domestic Violence Intervention Program, women are seventy times more likely to be killed in the two weeks after leaving an abusive relationship than at any other time during the relationship.

7. The third leading cause of homelessness among families is domestic violence, according to the National Coalition for The Homelessness. And, this is why many female victims don't leave the abusive relationship.

8. Nineteen percent of domestic violence involves a weapon.

9. The presence of a gun in a domestic violence situation increases the risk of homicide by five hundred percent.

10. Each year, ten million children are exposed to domestic violence. And this will no doubt affect these children, if you were to ask me, for the rest of their lives.

And, these are just a few of the sad, frightening, and preventable facts about domestic violence.

Domestic violence has been around for many decades. For example, when I was about five years old, there was a blind lady who used to visit her grandfather who lived right next-door to us every summer. Her name, as everybody around our neighborhood called her, was Baby Mae. She was young, and she looked to be in her mid-thirties. One day I asked my mother why was she blind, and Mama told me that her husband used to beat her in her face every time they got into a fight. Even as a kid, I felt sad and sorry for her every time I saw her because she couldn't see at all. In addition, and to all men especially, perpetuating domestic violence on women doesn't give you a macho image. Instead, this kind of behavior makes you look less than a macho man, even less than a dog, Roscoe for example. My daddy used to always say when I was a child that a man isn't a man if he stands up and fight a woman. Also, there was another animal that was very macho and more macho than any man probably ever will be, yet he showed the whole nation during the 1960s in a movie named for him that he had the utmost respect for women by protecting and not harming them. This animal was King Kong. King Kong was a gorilla that was taller than a five-story building. And, he was capable of crushing airplanes with his bare hands. After destroying a whole city one night, when he reached down and scooped up the beautiful Vina Fay Wray he didn't attempt to hurt her at all. Instead, she was the one who got him to calm down.

Now, Roscoe was real, and King Kong was fictional, but they both had one good characteristic in common; respect for females. Why does domestic violence keep happening? Ignorance. Readers, any psychologist will tell you that all behavior, especially human behavior, is learned. Therefore, I am asking that all parents, teachers, preachers, and all Americans start teaching and speaking against domestic violence to their children, students, and members as early as possible, and continue to do so until they can't. This is a war that all Americans need to join in together and fight against. Many people don't know any better than to indulge in domestic violence because they haven't been taught or trained properly not to do so.

So, let us all join in and do what the Bible tells us to do in Proverbs 22:6 which plainly states this,

"Train up a child in the way he should go: and when he is old, he will not depart from it."

People, let's start training.

And, may God bless us all.

Recommendations for Parents and Teachers

When Roscoe wouldn't fight the girl dog, Trixie, after just having been involved in two previous dog fights, Johnny Ray Thompson just couldn't believe it. So, he had to go and ask his daddy why his dog acted the way that he did.

Nevertheless, here are some ideas for some activities to do with your child or your students before, during, and after you have read this book together. But remember the most important thing is that your child or students have fun, enjoy reading and discussing this book, and get a good thorough understanding of the intended message that this book is conveying, domestic violence is wrong, and it is a crime. Also, make sure that your child or students understand that they can go to jail for this crime.

For Starters

A. Read the title aloud. Ask your child or students do they know what having good moral principles mean. If they don't, explain that it means having a nice and respectable way that a person or an animal conducts or carries his or herself in the presence of others.

B. Ask was Johnny Ray surprised that his dog didn't fight the last dog? Explain to your child or students why.

While Reading The Story

C.   Everything that Roscoe did was true. Ask your male child or students how would they handle a situation if a girl hit them first or would just reach over and take some of their food or other belongings.

D.   Ask your child or students how they think Johnny Ray felt when he first got Roscoe.

E.   Ask your child or students what's their favorite picture in this book and why.

After Reading This Book

F.   Ask your child or students questions about this story.

G.   How do they think Johnny Ray felt when Roscoe didn't fight Trixie a second time?

H.   How do they think he felt when Dennis called his dog a mutt?

I.   Has anyone ever teased you and called you chicken like Dennis did Johnny Ray trying to provoke you to do something that you really didn't want to do? If so, explain to them how to handle these situations.

Learning As They Go:

J. Make a list of some good advice with your child or students together, and that you have passed on to others.

K. Have your child or students to write a letter to their parents or grandparents, and ask them how they feel about Domestic Violence.

L. Take up all of the letters together and go to the post office and mail them.

M. As each student get a response from the parent or grandparent by mail, have him or her to read it aloud in class for discussion.

What Inspired The Author To Write The Book?

The author was inspired to write this book because of his own personal experiences. For example, as a small child he witnessed a lady who was blind coming to visit her grandfather, Mr. Turner Watts, who lived right next door to his family every summer in Mississippi. Later, when he asked his mother why the blind lady couldn't see, his mother told him that the lady, Miss Baby Mae, was blinded by her husband who would beat her in her face every time they got into a fight. In Addition, and on Sunday February 16,1992, the author's own nephew, Kenneth Undre Thompson, was shot to death by his own live-in girlfriend. At the time, Kenneth and his girlfriend had a nine-month old daughter. This child never got a chance to see and enjoy her father and he never got a chance to see and enjoy his daughter. Also, and on another Sunday February 20, 2005, the author had a cousin, Mr. Henry Handy who shot and killed his wife in the presence of their three children and then turned the gun on himself committing suicide. It was these senseless acts of violence and murder, along with many more of their ilk that continues today, that he says provoked him to write this book to bring awareness as early as possible to kids and adults about the facts and dangers of Domestic Violence.